RUMI

RUMI
DAY BY DAY

MARYAM MAFI

AMARYLLIS
An imprint of Manjul Publishing House

AMARYLLIS

An imprint of Manjul Publishing House Pvt. Ltd.
• C-16, Sector 3, Noida, Uttar Pradesh, 201301– India
Website: www.manjulindia.com

Registered Office:
• 2nd Floor, Usha Preet Complex, 42 Malviya Nagar,
Bhopal 462 003 – India

Distribution Centres
Ahmedabad, Bengaluru, Chennai, Hyderabad,
Kochi, Kolkata, Mumbai, Noida, Pune

This edition first published in India in 2026,
by arrangement with Red Wheel / Weiser LLC.

Cover design by Manjul Publishing House

ISBN 978-93-7317-335-1

Authorised for sale in the Indian Subcontinent only

Printed and bound in India by Parksons Graphics Pvt. Ltd.

Table of Contents

Introduction

In autumn 2012, my last book of Rumi poems had just been published and I was taking a break from translating. I met up with my friend Susan, who has always been a great inspiration, for a meal and to catch up after not having seen her for a long time. We spoke about how Rumi has influenced both our lives and how, in fact, he was responsible for our friendship. An avid meditator, Susan soon turned the conversation to meditation and how it had changed her life, and she suggested that I do a book of Rumi meditations! The idea greatly appealed to me as I, too, had been thinking of working on a new book that involved short, key mystic messages.

Rumi, Day by Day is a book of daily reflection in which the poems, sometimes just a single verse, have been scrupulously chosen from the six volumes of the *Massnavi*, which contains more than 25,000 verses. The *Massnavi*, unlike Rumi's spiritual love poems in the Divan-e Shams, is a book of teaching stories. His poetry, inspired by his spiritual master Shams, explores the ceaseless inner traveling that we must all engage in during our lifetime. This inner growth is a constant and endless movement. Our consciousness is challenged on a daily basis, and we are encouraged to rise up and meet those challenges with inner strength and, above all else, with love.

Rumi, Day by Day is thus not a romantic poetry book. Rather, it is a book that reminds us of many commonsense sayings, subtle nuances that our elders alluded to regularly but that, with time, we have lost. Rumi reminds us of these little nourishing gems, often with multiple meanings on many levels, each intended for a specific ear. One may wonder why Rumi appears to repeat himself, why we should focus on his aphorisms, the gist of which we may have heard in other, more modern contexts. Rumi indeed repeats himself, over and over again until his thoughts and wisdom are imprinted in our minds, our hearts, and our consciousness. One may find that many of these sayings come across as harsh, but Rumi has never been one to sugarcoat reality. Every day, our thoughts, our actions, and our inactions change our lives forever. To go through life fully aware of this process and its consequences at all times is second nature for Sufi masters; however, we can at best try to be touched by their wisdom and implement it in our daily lives. By referring to Rumi every day, we are reminding ourselves of the simplicity yet depth of life.

The Indian spiritualist and writer Jiddu Krishnamurti (1895–1986) once said that any effort at meditation is the denial of meditation, yet as conscious human beings we need to rise above who we think we are and to find our true selves. Although appearances are forever changing, the essence of things never changes, like the God essence that we all share in our hearts. *Rumi, Day by Day* is not a meditation book that aims to help us forget who and where we are; it is a book that brings us back to ourselves. As a realist, Rumi knew that we all must live on this earth at a particular time, and he helps us deal with our lives with clarity. He doesn't wish us to settle for an easily attained spirituality that elevates us one day and abandons us the next. He does not take us out of ourselves, but helps us reflect on the serious business of being present, of being aware of each moment, of experiencing each breath. Rumi repeatedly insists on avoiding bad company, people who are ignorant or otherwise negative. He is adamant about thinking positively while being aware of the negative influences that may surround us at any given moment. He warns us over and over again about the treacherous ego, telling us how to identify it even as it works in our subconsciousness, how to control it rather than deny it. He wants us to be aware of our own behavior, our reactions to events and people with whom we come into contact, and our thoughts about others and ourselves. In short, he wants us to live our lives on this earth with open eyes, with mindfulness, and ultimately with love.

I hope that we can take advantage of Rumi's brilliance, each in our own way, on a daily basis with this book and allow him to enter our hearts to enlighten our way back home to ourselves.

RUMI, DAY BY DAY

1.

Relationships are like farming,
if you don't plant the seed,
you'll have no crop to harvest.

2.

When you see a lover,
you see a beloved; he is both.
As the thirsty seek water,
water also seeks the thirsty.

3.

Stay aware and purposeful in your search,
for happiness is truly in the searching.

4.

Every contraction is naturally followed by an expansion;
every time you feel your heart shrivel
be confident that it will blossom in turn.

5.

Our mind is constantly defeated
and habitually surrenders
to our daily desires
steering us away
from our enchantment with God.

6.

What the fool only perceives in the end
the wise have observed from the beginning.

7.

How can I reach for the heavenly skies
when all day long I am bound up
in the pursuit of earthly profits,
fearful of losing everything,
unable to let joy into my life?

8.

Speech is both fire and nourishment
an endless bounty and at the same time
a ravaging pestilence.
Be wary of your speech.

9.

The wise do not look at "more" or "less,"
they know that both are
as transient as a flash flood.

10.

Sitting with a fool
is like sitting on a cold slab of stone,
soon he will steal all your warmth
and leave you with a chill to die from.

11.

Children tell many tales, some imaginary,
some graced with hidden guidance;
seek the treasure buried in the clutter.

12.

My body may seem meek but
my spirit does somersaults in the sky!

13.

Spotting faults in others is easy
and rehashing them, even easier,
but recognizing your own faults
is real mastery!

14.

The rich guard their possessions closely,
convinced that they own it all,
anxious that they may lose it one day.
Little do they know that it is all borrowed
and they are but momentary caretakers.

15.

How useless to know the value of all things
but to know nothing of one's own worth.

16.

Fear and anxiety
seize our hearts
when the object of our desire
is hidden from us.

17.

When you keep adding wood to the fire,
why should it ever die out?

18.

Sharing spiritual secrets
with the uninitiated has a limit.
The vastness of the sea can't be constrained
within the banks of a stream.

19.

Wealth is like seeds,
one must not plant them
in salt fields
where nothing grows.

20.

To love is to open the window of the heart,
reflecting the beauty of the one we love.
We must gaze steadily into our beloved's face
to open the path into our inner self.

21.

When I seek to please God,
I do so consciously, without any doubt.
When I carry a burden,
I know where I'm destined to go.
I am the moon and the Sun is my guide.

22.

Are you giving to charity
out of sincere love
or to compete with your neighbors?

23.

The blade of kindness is sharper than steel,
more unyielding than a surging army.

24.

Giving advice to a sleepy ignoramus
is like planting saplings in a field of salt.

25.

To arrive at clear water
one must first shovel through mud.

26.

The hostility of the wise
holds infinitely more value
than the kindness of fools.

27.

Foresight is choosing carefully between two paths.

28.

Sorrow engulfs when the ego
can't collect enough of the spoils.

29.

When it's easier to do evil
but you choose to do good,
you are a true hero.

30.

Death, like most phenomena,
will treat you the same way you have treated him;
with someone who's been friendly
he will be kind and amicable,
and with an enemy he will wage war.

31.

Don't be surprised
if those poisoned words you spoke
one day turn into snakes and scorpions
and grip you by the throat.

32.

Learn a vocation that will help you
through this world and the next.

33.

Jealousy arises from love,
no one can bear to see
his lover in company with another.

34.

Every true word is a seed to trap us,
for only the truth can bring peace to our hearts.

35.

The language of love
is not uttered in words.

36.

When you notice a fault in your neighbor,
search for the same in yourself.

37.

Isn't it ironic that we can't sacrifice any of our comforts
but how quickly we abandon the
One who provided them!

38.

Patience is the best prayer.

39.

If you want to ease your misery,
toss away those superficial facts
that you embrace as knowledge.

40.

Our soul and our spirit
are simply awareness,
the greater our sentience,
the more complete our days.

41.

Share your wisdom
even if your audience
seems disinterested at the time.

42.

If you must fight,
then choose an enemy
whom you can beat.

43.

Imperfection is the mirror of perfection;
opposites reveal each other.

44.

Exuberant joy, like inconsolable sorrow,
will pass sooner or later.
Stay aloof from both
as they will ultimately blow by.

45.

When you succeed in controlling
the words that you speak aloud,
the words that you speak to yourself
may then astonish you.

46.

The sweetness of joy is the fruit of the garden of sorrow;
until you have tasted the bitterness of loss,
you will not know the pleasure of contentment.

47.

When in real need,
even the forbidden
becomes allowed.

48.

To be jealous
of those more spiritually advanced than oneself
is a sign of immaturity and inexperience.

49.

Once a feeling enters your heart,
no matter where you run
it will always catch up with you.

50.

The sun can bathe filth with its light
but the sunlight will never be tarnished.

51.

The place that is placeless
where the light of God shines
has no present or past;
time does not exist there.

52.

When you become accustomed to grandeur
and someone steps on your pride,
you'll become their staunchest enemy.

53.

Be swift as an arrow when slaying
the adder of greed and the viper of lust
before they grow into merciless
dragons and devour you.

54.

If you can't completely free yourself
from all your worldly attachments,
at least try to shed some of them
to lessen the burden on your journey.

55.

Not until it turns into gold
does copper realize
what it had been before.
Not until the king finds his heart
does he realize how destitute
he had been until that moment.

56.

They say that it is experience that makes
one person superior to another,
but what about the child
whose startling insight can reveal mysteries
that an elder with a lifetime of experience
could never have gleaned?

57.

Midway means nothing to infinity.

58.

When totally immersed in pursuits that you love,
illness and pain won't distract you.

59.

Our body is only a cloak;
seek the one who has dressed you,
heed not the dress.

60.

I wonder why when a bird
clearly sees the trap laid out for her,
she's still drawn to fly straight in!

61.

The perfect speaker
is like a generous host
whose table is set
with a great variety of dishes
to suit every palate.

62.

When you yearn for truth,
you can be certain that truth also
yearns to be known by you.

63.

Don't you know
that if you feign sickness,
genuine sickness will seek you out?

64.

All the world's upheaval
arises from the dictates of "time."
When you free yourself from time's bondage,
you'll be astounded by
the timelessness of a higher order.

65.

You are a mystic pupil,
continue your search
with unquenchable thirst.
The arena of spirituality has no bounds;
abandon your preconceptions
about the ultimate state of being.
For you, it's all in your searching.

66.

Let us trust our inner sense
that may grasp a truth
invisible to our outer senses.

67.

Nothing is worse than ignorance,
to be sitting besides one's beloved
and not know how to lose
in the game of love!

68.

Choosing the middle path
is always a wise course,
but knowing the position of the "middle"
is a matter of perspective.
Water rushing in a stream
may only lap around the camel's knees,
but the mouse sees the same stream
as an unfathomable abyss.

69.

Don't you see that if you
continue to mistreat a loyal friend,
before long you'll see him
coiling up into a venomous snake?

70.

Those with warm open hearts
also tend to have generous hands.

71.

To be showered with pearls from the sun
and still grope for a lantern!

72.

If you are prone to incessantly arguing,
tying up your life in useless knots,
you will then squander the rest of your days
trying to undo those futile knots.

73.

Our body and soul are one,
yet how amazing that our body
may not necessarily know our soul!

74.

Most things that happen in this world
are a chain around one person's ankles,
yet a sweet release for another.

75.

Do you want him to be sweet with you?
Then be sweet with him and
look at him with loving eyes.

76.

Like the foolish owls
we made enemies with falcons,
now we are doomed forever
to live amongst the ruins.

77.

No one knows how spirit moves our bodies,
but because of our movement,
we know that spirit exists.

78.

Infinite kinds of tempting seeds
lie scattered before us,
and we, like insatiable birds,
cannot control our hunger
and fly straight into the net.

79.

Holding grudges and being vengeful
only lead one astray and obscure
one's true purpose in life.

80.

We know instinctively
that behind every movement
there is a Mover.
Our eyes can't see Him,
but we can begin to fathom Him
from the tracks He leaves behind.

81.

It is God's privilege to test us anytime He fancies so that He can reveal what lies deep in our hearts.

82.

When you become besotted with a thought, no one can point out to you its negative sides.

83.

For the mystic
to die is not to perish,
it is to merge with eternity.

84.

It is in hope of the fruit
that a farmer plants a tree.
The tree then, is born of the fruit
rather than the fruit from the tree.

85.

You can't even control the graying of your beard,
how can you expect to control
any right or wrong done in this world?

86.

True mystics become alchemists
and can turn objects into silver and gold;
thus these precious metals no longer
hold a grip over their souls.

87.

The master told his pupils,
I will never ask you
to bring me precious gifts
but I *will* ask you to become
worthy of *receiving* gifts.

88.

Those longing looks
that the bird casts on the sprinkled seeds
are indeed a chain around its feeble feet.

89.

This world is a simple wine jug,
and the heart, a flowing stream.
This world is an enclosed room,
and the heart, an open city of wonders!

90.

Our body is a veil like straw covering
the surface of the water.
How much longer can mere straw
continue to cover the magnificent sea?

91.

Anger is a spark from the flames of hell;
put it out quickly with your inner light
before it consumes you in its blaze.

92.

When someone complains
about an ill-tempered person,
you know that the complainer
is bad-tempered himself,
for the truly amiable are
infinitely tolerant.

93.

A tradesman's tools
may seem as inanimate objects to you,
but to him, they are
his most cherished companions.

94.

Our words and actions
are the perfect mirror
to our inner selves.

95.

The urge to do wrong is like fire,
its beautiful color pleasing to the eye;
yet hidden inside there's a darkness
that only becomes apparent
once the flames are out.

96.

Imagine someone saying to God,
"I did this evil act just to test You!"

97.

In this world opposites
are always at each other's throats;
where there are no opposites,
there is harmony.

98.

Like a blind camel being led by its harness,
everything moves toward that which pulls it;
sometimes in the right direction, sometimes not.
Focus on who's pulling you, not on the harness.

99.

The merchant with a delicate nature
who's always hesitant to risk a trade
will never lose his capital, nor ever profit.
If you want to come into the light,
you must be in love with the flame.

100.

Rewarding an evil person
with knowledge and skills
is like giving a murderer a dagger.

101.

When an ignorant person
comes into money and fame,
he will eventually reveal his true self
by being either pathetically stingy
or unreasonably generous.

102.

Why do you persist with this idle talk
knowing that the only way
to answer a fool is with silence?

103.

While you are basking in the joy of spring,
remember the cold rusty autumn.
The sun's beautiful ascent in the morning
is only followed by its setting at dusk.

104.

The detailed formulas of chemistry,
the sciences of astronomy, medicine,
and philosophy are all well and good,
but the science of Truth
has its only home
in the heart of the lover.

105.

My God,
You are the keeper of secrets;
don't hide from me my faults,
but do conceal the difficulties
that lie ahead in my future endeavors
lest I lose heart and never try.

106.

This world and its inhabitants
share the same attribute: fickleness.

107.

Has anyone ever seen
two prophets opposing one another
or stealing each other's miracles?

108.

The ego is remarkably clever and astute;
its holy ground is this earth;
it's best to bury it here.

109.

When love demands sacrifices,
do not take offense; even kiss the snake
if you want to behold the Treasure.

110.

God has graced every soul with His light.
Some have opened their arms
to behold it more than others.
If you have never felt love,
you have no share of His light.

111.

Our eyes are minuscule,
weighing a mere ounce,
yet the light they project
spans all the heavens.

112.

There are two types of intellect:
one is kindled by books and learning,
while the other is gifted to us
by the grace of Spirit.

113.

We live in a world illuminated
by the sun and the moon;
if you poke your head down a well,
don't complain that you're in the dark!

114.

When you upset your friends
with your self-centered boasting,
don't be surprised if they turn on you.

115.

Your tooth is part of you,
but pull it out if it's rotten
and preserve the rest of your body
before it is fraught with decay.

116.

Reason is a chain around the ego's neck.

117.

Deviant people remind one
of a ship without an anchor,
defenseless in the face of a storm.

118.

We can amass a fortune
and build ourselves
the most advanced ships,
but where can we find
a captain like Noah?

119.

Why must the trees' yellowing leaves
indicate old age and uselessness?
Why can't they signify
maturity and wholeness?

120.

The eggs of a sparrow may resemble those of a snake
and the seeds of a pear may seem like those of an apple,
but the difference between them is boundless.

121.

Silence is a sea,
while the stream is busy chatter.
The sea will find you,
but you must first arise from the stream.

122.

I wonder why a jug of wine
can create such rosy exhilaration,
while the passion for Truth
leaves us totally unblemished!

123.

The true mystic has merged with the truth;
he is only a mirror to reflect others.
If you spit at him, you're spitting at yourself,
if you see an ugly face, it's your very own,
and if you see the reflection of Jesus and Mary,
that is you too.
The selfless mystic merely reflects you.

124.

Love murmurs in my ear that to be hunted
is infinitely more enviable than to be the hunter.

125.

The sweet pleasure of reaching one's destination
is amplified by the suffering
one has endured during the journey.

126.

If you need to seek counsel,
choose someone who's joyful
and high-spirited so that he can
evoke the same in you.

127.

It's futile to regret the past
which is gone, irretrievable,
its company fleeting as dust.

128.

Harboring friendship with fools
is like being your own enemy.

129.

Before raising a new building,
the old one must first be torn down.
Before stitching a new garment,
the tailor must first cut the precious cloth.

130.

The true mystic respects the value of time
and never puts anything off till tomorrow.

131.

Don't imagine that your eyes only see
because of their mechanism;
how could optics possibly account for
the vivid images in your dreams?

132.

To achieve purity of heart
we must acknowledge our every action,
for each move that we make
will have a repercussion
reflecting back on us.

133.

A person is like a running stream;
when muddied by the ego's greed,
one can't see clearly the treasure that lies
not so deep beneath the surface.

134.

If we think that we know God from His creations,
it is not God that we know but only His creations.

135.

I pray to be liberated from the chains of jealousy,
to be set free from worldly attachments;
instead I want to fill my heart with matters of spirit
to help me resist the distractions of the outside world.

136.

Kneeling in submission before another
only serves to enslave him,
for once you stop your prostrations,
he will feel helpless, lost, and abandoned.

137.

Pride is that poisoned wine
we so easily get drunk on.

138.

The ego is like a ladder;
the higher you climb,
the harder you will fall.

139.

Everything that is created
disguises a hidden purpose.
A potter creates a jug
not just to fill it with wine
but also for its beauty.
A calligrapher writes out his lines
not just for the exquisiteness of the script
but to also convey a meaning.

140.

Depending on the breadth of our vision,
we are each regularly exposed to certain
apparent as well as hidden mysteries of life.

141.

The higher one's aspiration and commitment,
the stronger one's longing and motivation.

142.

We have an enemy within called the ego
who prevents us from using our mind intelligently.
It hides deep within our heart
and emerges with regularity
to challenge and consume our will.

143.

God told Moses that He loved him greatly.
Moses asked why, so he could nurture the trait
that made him so lovable to God.
God said, you are for me like an innocent child
who takes solace in his mother's arms
even though he might be furious with her,
for he knows that there is no better refuge.

144.

Acquired knowledge can lead
to both wisdom and delusion,
like a fruit that, when ripened,
can turn either bitter or sweet.

145.

In life we'll find those who are
pure, delicate souls and others
who are dark as coal.
It's imperative that we separate the two,
like dividing the wheat from the chaff.

146.

Our wealth will not keep us company outside our palaces;
our friends will stay with us only till the
hour of our passing;
only our deeds are loyal enough to accompany us
to our graves.

147.

No one seeks their beloved
unless they too are being sought.

148.

For the jester, life's a sequence of jokes
while for the wise, jokes comprise true wisdom;
don't belittle them out of hand,
for jokes can impart valuable lessons.

149.

Your true self is sheer intelligence
and the rest of you, only appearance;
don't lose sight of your true self,
don't waste your time chasing trivial
yet unobtainable goals.

150.

Lust is like drug addiction;
it strangles the intellect and
confuses the mind.

151.

Speak gently when you offer criticism,
but don't be so soft as to sacrifice the truth.

152.

Acknowledging a blessing
is sweeter than the blessing itself.
It is the giving of thanks
that brings us closer to God.

153.

Every single part in this world
longs for its counterpart.

154.

For the snake, venom is life,
while for us, it is our end.

155.

When, every day, you scrape a little soil
from a mountain and don't replace it,
one day there'll be no mountain left.

156.

When a person walks by
draped with priceless robes and jewels,
you may wonder, does silk
increase one's intelligence?

157.

Patience is the hands and feet of foresight;
together they provide a safe passage through life.

158.

A land bird and a waterbird
may look similar, but in reality
they're like oil and water,
each faithful only to its own essence.

159.

Man is like a sailboat
dependent on the wind
that God allows to blow.

160.

Beware of the one to whom
you've been generous and kind;
some friendships are like sharp swords
leaving a swath of suspicion and deceit.

161.

Foresight requires diligence;
a measure of doubt
to guard against letdown and hurt.

162.

How can we stoop to be unfaithful
when even dogs cherish fidelity!

163.

Cut it from the roots when you feel
a negative thought descending;
learn to control your soul's contraction
and diligently water the sapling
of your soul's expansion.

164.

Why are we never satisfied?
In summertime we pray
for the coolness of winter,
and when winter finally arrives,
we long for the smothering heat
that comes with summer.

165.

Indecision is the prison
where the soul is kept captive.

166.

An unkind word from a friend
is infinitely more hurtful to one's soul
than if uttered by a stranger.

167.

From our first breath to our last
life's a series of tests;
don't be too proud
if you've passed a few.

168.

From encountering the parts
one may grasp the whole.
From knowing the opposite
one can conceive the original.

169.

Let's cleanse our minds
of all our acquired knowledge,
and when we're back to knowing nothing,
perhaps then we can aspire
to be enlightened by the truth.

170.

In our hearts
there is a blazing light
that belongs neither
to the East nor to the West.

171.

Why do you run scattershot
begging for answers
when you are the essence
of all meaning?

172.

When ill temper becomes habitual,
the friend who tries to warn you
will become the target of your wrath.

173.

Sell your brains
and buy yourself
spiritual bewilderment!

174.

The answers to all your questions
are found in the same place
where you turn to in prayer
in times of need.

175.

How can the wolf
hope to find the sheep
if their shepherd is God?

176.

When you focus on their outward form,
you will see only differences between
the Muslim, the Christian, and the Jew.
Why not zoom in on the inner light
that they all share?

177.

Where were Moses and Jesus
when the sun first nourished all of creation?
Where were Adam and Eve
when the Creator was first aiming
His arrow at conception?

178.

You possess the elixir of alchemy within,
use it to transmute your enemies into friends.
Once you are beatified, you are able
to reflect the beauty of the Beloved.

179.

You are not alone, my dear friend,
you are the world, the endless sea.

180.

Embrace silence
so that you can hear
the master speak of things
you may never find
in books or idle talk.

181.

Be charitable with people for God's delight
and for your own peace of mind
so that your heart is cleansed of hurt
and you are forever surrounded by friends.

182.

When you are perpetually yearning
and constantly searching for Spirit,
you will, in time, conquer all obstacles.

183.

If you want to glean the mystics' wisdom
and learn how they've conquered their ego,
you need to sit with them,
you need to keep them company.

184.

Your wealth, your expertise,
in fact everything you have,
did they not all at first
begin with a single thought?

185.

When you wish for something,
be mindful of what you can tolerate.
A straw mat cannot withstand
the weight of a mountain.
The sun nourishes our world,
but if it were to come too close,
it would scorch us all.

186.

This world is a mountain;
our own actions, their echoes
forever rebounding back on us.

187.

A fruit is reflective
of the soil it grows in
like our thoughts, which reflect
the secrets buried in our hearts.

188.

Everyone can distinguish
between kindness and anger,
but only the mystic can see that
within the folds of kindness anger often lurks,
and, buried in anger's heart, kindness lies in wait.

189.

Our beauty is hidden in our words!

190.

When your heart is bewildered by divine love,
there will be no more secrets to unravel.

191.

We easily get drunk on our worldly passions,
our social standing, even our daily bread,
and if we lose even one, we are crippled
with the most dreadful hangover.

192.

Relying on disloyal people
is as risky as crossing
a broken-down bridge.

193.

We all have the attribute of cruelty within us,
but the ruthless cannot squelch it for long;
without our intervention sooner or later
they're bound to reveal their true self.

194.

Being afflicted with illness evokes compassion,
but being plagued by thoughtlessness
only inflicts pain and sorrow
on one's innocent companions.

195.

Generosity toward one's family
isn't extraordinary;
it's the natural order of life.

196.

No one wants to cultivate hateful relationships
so gravitate toward intelligent people,
and avoid the egocentric, for they will instinctively
burden you with their cynicism.

197.

If only I could clear the ego's mist blinding my sight,
I could behold the endless sea in a single drop.

198.

The real master is beyond
the daily affairs of the world,
he's simply a pen held by God's fingers.

199.

When thirsty for spiritual life,
don't settle for just a sip;
stay with your thirst and you'll see
how the heavens will open their doors
to the water of life!

200.

We always find hope after despair,
the sun always rises
after the darkest part of the night.

201.

Short or tall, young or old
means nothing to my soul.

202.

In my heart
there's a vast garden
full of lush roses
where wilting and atrophy
do not occur.

203.

For criminals prison is a temple,
it's the only place where they remember God.

204.

Often beloveds jealously hide
their desire and longing
while their lovers declare their love
with the sound of a hundred
drums and trumpets!

205.

Cast off your disdain for death
and you'll see that it's not the end
but only a disguise
for a welcoming celebration.

206.

You stand knee deep in a stream
and still ask every passerby for a drink!

207.

Appearances are fallible,
clear water can be bitter or sweet,
but we will not know for certain
unless we take a drink.

208.

How can the monkey
who can only mimic
know our true intentions?

209.

If you need proof of the sun's existence,
don't turn your back on its light.

210.

To be a fair judge, you'll want to hear
all sides of a dispute and not allow the cries
of only one claimant to form your judgment.

211.

Stop trying to be shrewd
and allow yourself to be bewildered
because shrewdness leads to skepticism,
but when you are bewildered,
you'll be gifted the clarity of sight.

212.

In the desert, a true friend can be a guiding star;
keep your eyes focused on him,
don't stir up the dust, blinding yourself.

213.

The devil and the ego are of the same essence,
both are jealous of man and forever seek his ruin.

214.

When you are ready to hear the truth,
even the pebbles on the ground
are eager to spread the news.

215.

Mystics have nothing to do
with the material world,
they accumulate no savings
but forever reap profits.

216.

Everything in creation
is intended to relieve a need.
Everything that grows,
grows because someone, somewhere,
awaits it.

217.

When an ignorant chicken invites a camel
into his chicken coop, what else can he expect
but a collapsed roof and a ruined home?

218.

Open your eyes to his soul
before you decide
to sit with him as a friend.

219.

If you're faced with misfortune, welcome it
for heaven may have sent it to shield you
from a worse calamity lurking in the shadows.

220.

While you soar in prosperity,
seize the chance to be generous.

221.

Savor every moment of grace
when you sit and listen
at the feet of a true friend.

222.

A child who has never tasted a fresh apple
will not easily relinquish his rotten onion.

223.

If you are pricked by a thorn,
remember that it was you
who planted the rosebush.
If you find yourself wrapped
in exquisite silken robes,
remember that it was also you
who spun that skein of silk.

224.

Anger that you allow to rise up in your heart
is a flame that grows into an inferno
devouring you and all that lies in your path.

225.

Found guilty, you may contest your guilt,
but for certain you are paying for a crime
that you committed elsewhere at some other time.
Punishment never resembles the crime.
When you harvest a fruit, does it look like the seed?

226.

The sweet offerings of this life
are but an illusion, as tenuous
as a fine mist in the cool morning air.
Use foresight to select aims
that have substance and surety.

227.

To pause and ponder is a Godly trait
as opposed to rushing headlong,
which occurs in the devil's realm.
Even dogs, before eating, first sniff
the dry bread you throw before them!

228.

An old person's feet
may not carry him far,
but his wisdom enables him to soar
to the skies far and beyond.

229.

Leaves on trees may look the same,
but their fruits are totally different.
People in a market walk alongside each other,
one may be anguished with a broken heart
and the other soaring in private delight.

230.

Walking in this world
with knowledge of a higher realm
is like traversing a vast, lush meadow
in painfully tight shoes!
Someone who sees you from afar
might think you were cavorting in heaven,
while all you can think of
is how to free yourself
from your suffocating state.

231.

Our body is a small, crammed house
where our soul cringes uncomfortably.
Our Creator annihilates this hovel
and builds a palace in its place.

232.

What is love?
A sea of nonexistence
both tranquil and calamitous
where the mind
does not dare enter.

233.

To imagine that what our mind
conceives as our world
is all there is of God's work
is to believe that the light of the sun
is the sun itself.

234.

How can a drop of water challenge the sea?
Will it obliterate itself out of sheer hubris?

235.

When we express our kindness,
it's tarnished with sorrow and pity,
but when God shows benevolence,
it's joyous and guilt free.

236.

The perfect master no longer exists,
his being has dissolved into spirit,
like candlelight before the sun,
invisible yet able to set alight
the bale of cotton that rests nearby.

237.

Where else but where my beloved is
could I think of as home?

238.

When we are touched by Beauty,
we can discern heaven
even in the belly of a dungeon.

239.

To remain dependent
on frivolous attachments is a living death.
Only when I free myself from my ego's cravings,
can I hope to live eternally.

240.

I do not need to take lessons in how to love,
the face of my beloved is my schooling.

241.

I may seem quiet and reposed,
but my silent proclamations of love
roar out to the heavenly spheres
where my Beloved lies in wait.

242.

What you acquire for little cost
you will part with, with equal disdain
like a hungry child,
quick to swap a pilfered gem
for a warm loaf of bread.

243.

It is Love
that spins our souls aloft.
It is Love
that exhorts even the mountains to dance.

244.

Absolute good like absolute evil
does not exist.
Everything is relative and situational.
We can only hope
that our wisdom may guide us.

245.

Let's not mistake the flames of love
for normal fire; far from it!
They are light upon light upon light.

246.

When you hear a mother cursing her child,
take no notice, for it's not the child
but the devil inside she's cursing.

247.

The devil and the ego,
like angels and intelligence,
are quintessentially the same
but with two separate faces.

248.

We are never confronted with a task
that denies us our free will.

249.

How can we apprehend what transpires
inside someone's heart
if all we hear is cheap chatter?

250.

A painting is bound by
the artist and his brush,
helpless and with no voice
like an infant in the womb.

251.

Those with knowledge seek certainty,
but the one who is certain
yearns for insight.

252.

My pen rushes to transcribe my thoughts,
but it disintegrates in my hand
when I come to the topic of love.
How inadequate are words
to love and the plight of the lover!

253.

When our inner eye is blind,
what other impression than heat
can we expect from the sun?

254.

"Division" is forever on the prowl
seeking out kinships to rend and tear.

255.

Intelligence is man's anchor in life;
cleave to intelligent people
if you seek stability and refuge.

256.

Our wings are our ambitions and aspirations.

257.

When love strikes,
nothing can help the love-struck
but love!

258.

All of God's creatures are created in pairs
in love
pulling toward each other like magnets.

259.

If you incessantly regret your actions,
soon there'll be nothing
that you won't regret.

260.

Day and night may seem like warring opposites,
but they share a dual purpose;
they need and complete each other.
Without the night we have no respite
and will be spent on each new day.

261.

When I'm with the one I love,
even crouched in a dark, hostile cave
I feel like I am not of this world.

262.

Nothingness is where God's workshop lies,
where all His treasures are hidden,
but if you're a slave to your own mind,
you'll never fully grasp this truth.

263.

Fall in love with love;
let yourself succumb until you're
but a shadow who's fallen for the sun.

264.

How can I keep my love a secret?
It's like trying to conceal fire
by wrapping it in cotton!

265.

I aim to hide love's secrets,
but she pulls at my ear
and challenges me to try.
Like wine in a cask,
she lies still, but apparent as life
she's hidden in our essence,
silent yet ecstatic.

266.

We're all made of flesh and bone,
where we differ is our virtues.
We may think we know each other,
but truly we are a mystery.

267.

The company of good friends
creates the graciousness of a rose garden
even if one is in the middle of a desert.

268.

The devil's hallmark is to stir up doubt.

269.

To pray and fast,
to go on pilgrimages,
to give alms, and
to resist jealousy
are the gems
in our hearts.

270.

Anger is hell,
and to survive, it demands an enemy,
for kindness only annihilates it.

271.

We can only hope to catch
a glimpse of people's inner light
through their actions and words,
and even then it remains an enigma,
but the perfect mystic's inner light
cannot be contained within him
for he does not follow the patterns
trod by other men.

272.

If you are willing to taste the wine
served at the invisible house of the Friend,
slowly, slowly love will draw you there.

273.

The only thing in life
worth chasing is love,
yet how can anyone catch love?
One's only chance is to surrender
and become love's prey.

274.

The undiscerning man wastes his life
attempting to collect friends
like a spider snares flies in a web,
but as his life rushes past,
one by one, his prey slip through the web
leaving him empty in his solitude.

275.

When you stop imitating others,
you'll be dazzled by the light of truth
in all things that you do.

276.

Love says, come hover near my window
abandon your home, forsake being the candle,
instead learn how to savor being the moth.

277.

Our life is a bag of gold coins
and every day we spend a little.

278.

If you're wondering why he's so in love,
you'll have to borrow his eyes and
look upon his beloved with his sight.

279.

The handsome peacock is indeed impressive,
but don't just envy his beautiful feathers,
take a good look at his feet too.

280.

Jealousy and the evil eye may be invisible,
but they are powerful enough
to turn our lives upside down.

281.

God's mercy is mightier than His wrath!

282.

I can seat a hundred guests at my table,
but I can't convince two power-hungry men
to sit together for one moment.

283.

Adverse thoughts
are like fingernails flaked with poison
that we use to scratch
our innocent souls.

284.

Only when I realize my limitations
can I hope to rise above them
and glimpse my endless possibilities.

285.

Our souls are like the city air;
when our ego rises, like dust from the street,
our eyes are veiled from the sun.

286.

If you need myriad reasons
to describe and understand God,
then turn to philosophers;
the mystic lover needs no reasoning
for he loves God because of God.

287.

The Sun does not need the moon and the stars
to bear witness to its existence.

288.

Truly our enemies are our cure and our balm,
to free ourselves from their grasp
we take refuge in God,
but our friends with whom we mostly have fun
only distract us from Him.

289.

Vengeance is the perfect workshop for anger
where the source of deceit and delusion is nourished.

290.

To ask anything of God but God alone
is to invite spiritual bankruptcy.

291.

It is said that we must be kind to three people:
the prosperous one who's lost his wealth,
the cherished boss who's fallen from grace,
and the scholar who's misunderstood by the masses.

292.

Our bodies may be separate,
but there's a clear path between our hearts.
Two lamps may not be attached at the base,
but the light they project is as one.

293.

The treasures of creation dwell in nonexistence
and, at each moment,
Spirit reveals something new.

294.

Our own actions are the most loyal messengers;
if noble, they will eternally proclaim our good name;
if base, like slithering worms,
they will forever pollute our grave.

295.

Are you aware that you're carrying
a basketful of bread on your head
and still begging at every door?

296.

Relentlessly a lover searches for his beloved;
once he finds her, he loses himself,
as his essence dissolves into hers.

297.

Justice is knowing how to use
a blessing in the right place.

298.

When you taste the primeval wine of love,
you will never rest until you taste it again.

299.

If you think your search for the lovers is over,
if you think you've reached your purpose,
think again;
the arena of the heart is so vast,
it will overwhelm even the seven skies.

300.

I know that I am now poor,
but I will never be impoverished.
Do not sneer at my tattered clothes,
my spirit is eternally rejuvenating.

301.

Jesus was asked what was the most
daunting force in the world,
"God's wrath, even hell shivers in fear of it."
How can we avoid it, he was asked,
"Control your anger."

302.

Do not ask my physical body
about what lies in my heart!

303.

Were I in control of my consciousness,
it would not forsake me while I sleep.
Since I have no reign over my dreams,
how amazing that I swagger with self-importance!

304.

Love is coquettish and proud,
she will only accept you
if you buy into her flirtations.
She's loyal and expects loyalty in return,
she turns her gaze from the treacherous.

305.

Green leaves may look lush and full of vigor,
but what's the use if the roots are rotten.

306.

Don't be lured
by your companion's easy knowledge.
Wait to see if he keeps his promises.

307.

Talk is the extinguishing of the mind;
when talk begins, the mind is spent.
It is in silence that the soul is nourished.
Spend less on talk
and keep your mind sharp and clear.

308.

Can we ever comprehend the perfect master?
Can the darkest night ever know the light of day?
Can the helpless fly
ever witness the mighty wind?

309.

Greed throws our benchmarks out of whack
and leads us to forsake moderation.
It's indeed a cunning adversary
that gathers all to itself.

310.

Our aching for God is His guarantee.

311.

Diligently we collect and store our harvest
unaware that hungry mice
empty our coffers every day.
The ego operates in like fashion,
silently, with devastating effect.

312.

When you learn to live in love,
I will become your slave.

313.

The Sufi lives in the moment;
tomorrow is but a mirage
for those who walk
on the spiritual path.

314.

I linger behind the curtain, knowing
that anything my beloved does, it is I myself doing,
for he has become me and I, him.

315.

What is pride other than
inattentiveness to the truth
staying frozen, oblivious
to the rising sun.

316.

Have you ever seen a person
writing on a page already filled with words
or planting saplings where trees already grow?
Better to be a blank sheet, better the virgin soil,
so the hand of Spirit may leave fresh traces.

317.

A lover asked her beloved
who does he love better, she or himself?
"I've lost myself in you, my being is now
filled with your being, all that is left of me
are the bare letters of my name."

318.

A gardener will show a few apples
as proof of his crop.
A farmer will bring a handful of wheat
as an exhibit of his harvest.
We've been shown a few small blessings
in our lives, so that we may well wonder
what God has in store.

319.

How long are we going to busy ourselves
scribbling prose and poetry, divulging secrets?
Just for one day let us try silence!

320.

Let us live in such a manner
that on Judgment Day
our actions, speaking for themselves,
shall vouch for our inner selves.

321.

Help a master, even with the most trivial of matters,
and you'll mostly be helping yourself,
for truly he has no need of your feeble efforts.

322.

We can't open a locked door without a key.
We can't expect God to offer His blessing
unless we long for Him,
unless we hunger for Him.

323.

Contentment is a treasure,
but not every man is content.
To know our limitations and
not foolishly aspire to the unattainable
will keep us in a state of grace.

324.

The hypocrite's apology
is a sackful of empty words,
repulsive and far from the heart.

325.

Those golden yellow leaves on the apple tree
may hold your gaze, but why not instead
focus on the apples ripe for picking?

326.

A poisonous snake can be lethal,
but a venomous friend
can condemn you to eternal fire!

327.

How can we confine love with mere words?
Can we count the drops of water in the sea?

328.

When you come by a mill wheel,
can you see the water that turns it?
When you see dust whirling in the air,
can you feel the wind that stirs it?
Let's search out the causes and
not content ourselves with the surface effects.

329.

When you finally learn to practice patience,
don't be so proud;
remember who taught you patience in the first place.

330.

If you're in doubt choosing
between two actions, remember
this is an example of free will,
and if you later regret your choice,
it may nevertheless
steer you in the right direction.

331.

You spend half your life in worry
and the other half in regret.
Don't squander your life with remorse;
find a more positive occupation,
and if you truly have nothing better to do,
then what loss are you regretting?

332.

When the essence has become one with the flower,
it matters not if you smell the flower or the essence.

333.

What else but love can quiet our temptations?
Is love not a muzzle on temptation's gaping maw?

334.

Why do we sell ourselves so short?
Why do we seek our innate knowledge in books?
How do we become so easily satisfied with
just a little sweet?
Is it because we don't know that we are a sea of wisdom
and that the whole of existence has been created
for our sake?

335.

Savor your sorrowful heart, be gentle and sweet;
think of it as a cloud nourishing the garden with its rain.
Welcome your sorrow for it may hold the secret
to unforeseen wisdom, and even if it doesn't,
you'll learn to smile in the face of adversity.

336.

Doubt forever thirsts for certainty.

337.

Oh God, I beg of You
to bestow upon me
that state of being
where I can speak with You
without words.

338.

To ward off misfortune,
the answer is not to create more harm
but to be tolerant and forgiving.

339.

To speak the same language is a blessing,
to be misunderstood is like being imprisoned.
Yet a Turk and a Hindu
may understand one another far better
than two Turks, who share the same language.

340.

Oh God, in the very beginning
You granted my soul one drop of knowledge;
please won't You allow me to connect
with Your entire sea of grace?

341.

Religious zealots live in fear of doomsday,
while enlightened Sufis live forever free
from such foolish anxieties.

342.

Be kind to the one who happens
to glance at your beautiful face.
How will he ever survive
forever severed from that beauty?

343.

It is sweet for me to die
hoping to be reunited with you in eternal bliss,
for what need do I have for this beating heart
that smolders with the bitterness of our separation?

344.

Be a friend to others, don't be a churl,
and you'll see how even the bitterest of fruit
will taste sweeter than honey.

345.

Love wants nothing to do
with the everyday affairs of men.
Love's only intention
is to catch the lover!

346.

One should only share secrets with those
who know how to keep them.
To tell a secret to the unappreciative
is to squander that secret.

347.

For an eternity I was but a speck
floating in air, carefree.
I may not remember that buoyant state
as I pass from day to day,
but in my sleep I still travel there
and am free from the dregs of this world.

348.

Were we to know the outcome of events,
why would we dally in their pursuit?
So please God, hide from us what may ensue
so that we may act according to our fate.

349.

It is justice to use
a scarce supply of water
to nourish a young sapling
but injustice to splash that water
at the roots of a shriveled, dead scrub.

350.

When I find myself faltering between two paths
is that not a sign of free will?
How often have you seen a vacillator,
hands and feet firmly bound
by his own indecision?

351.

It is futile for me to ponder how
to plunge to the bottom of the ocean
or to soar to the seventh sky.
I could fruitfully wonder, though,
how to travel to one town or another.
Hesitation is acceptable only
when there's a possibility of action;
otherwise it should be scorned.
Let us lay less blame on fate
for our action or immobility
and instead take a deep look within
to understand our decisions.

352.

When we have little strength to fight,
better to abstain from confrontation
and quickly take flight.

353.

Be a friend and cultivate
a circle of amity;
without true friends none of us
can survive for long.

354.

I am content to walk alone,
but to walk in company with others
adds vigor and passion to the journey.

355.

The ant, spotting a grain of wheat,
trembles with excitement.
He carries it greedily, fearful of losing it,
oblivious to the massive blessing
of the whole crop that lies before him.

356.

My inner sight is what gives me substance,
all else is just flesh and blood.
I am only what my inner eye perceives.

357.

Before God no heart is dismissed.
His intentions are not profit bound.

358.

The one who spots the line
before spotting the bait
is the ultimate winner in life.

359.

The positive aspect of wayward friends
is that they teach us patience,
which in turn opens our hearts.
Look at the moon, how it grows brighter
as it patiently tolerates the dark night.
Or the beautiful rose, which has become
so much more fragrant
despite being encumbered with thorns.

360.

When our eyes learn to perceive higher truth,
they will see beyond the visible.
In a grain of sand,
they will observe the everlasting sun.
In a drop of water,
the infinite sea.

361.

Show me the one
who has fallen in love with love
for love's sake only!

362.

To share a path with a companion
warms the heart and promises sanctuary,
but, looking more closely,
our companion is himself the path.

363.

When you arrive at a feast of friends,
tread lightly and tend toward silence.
To exhibit the poise of a master,
don't make an exhibit of yourself.

364.

Love is reckless and carefree;
small, trifling minds seek profit,
but true lovers lavish everything on love
and never expect benefits in return.

365.

Keeping company with intelligent friends
is a hedge against misfortune.
Intelligence is like a lamp,
the more one cultivates enlightened people,
the more one can bask
in their warm, illuminating glow.

Acknowledgments

I would like to thank my old friend and colleague, Norman Ware, who thanks to Google, came back into my life after an absence of more than twenty-five years, just when I needed him most. His superb editorial skills, as well as his heartfelt understanding of the subject matter, have made this joint endeavor an absolute pure joy.

Index

The poems were selected from Karim Zamani's edition of Rumi's *Massnavi,* six volumes, Tehran: Etela'at Publishers, 1998.

In this listing, M stands for the *Massnavi*; the Roman numerals indicate the volume within the six volumes of Rumi's works; and the Arabic numbers are the verse numbers.

1. MIII 2392
2. MI 1740
3. MIII 2302
4. MIII 3735
5. MIV 1246
6. MIII 2197
7. MI 411
8. MI 1700
9. MI 2289
10. MIII 2597
11. MIII 2602
12. MIV 1882
13. MIII 2629
14. MIII 2639
15. MIII 2649
16. MI 3625
17. MI 3704
18. MI 3810
19. MI 3718
20. MVI 3096
21. MI 3809
22. MI 3717
23. MI 3989
24. MIV 2264
25. MII 1831
26. MII 1877
27. MIII 2842
28. MIII 3284
29. MIII 3298
30. MIII 3439
31. MIII 3475
32. MII 2594
33. MII 2643
34. MII 2736
35. MI 113
36. MII 3034
37. MII 3075
38. MII 3145

39. MII 3201
40. MII 3326
41. MIII 3611
42. MIII 3625
43. MI 3210
44. MIII 3698
45. MIII 3747
46. MIII 3752
47. MII 3416
48. MII 3429
49. MIII 3774
50. MII 3411
51. MIII 1151
52. MII 3466
53. MII 3472
54. MII 3525
55. MII 3474
56. MIII 1541
57. MII 3542
58. MIII 1604
59. MIII 1610
60. MIII 1648
61. MIII 1895
62. MIII 4442
63. MIII 1580
64. MIII 2074
65. MIII 1960
66. MIII 1995
67. MIII 3781
68. MII 3531
69. MIII 3787
70. MII 3640
71. MVI 3390
72. MII 3733
73. MI 8
74. MIV 66
75. MIV 74
76. MII 3747

77. MIV 155
78. MI 374
79. MIV 112
80. MIV 153
81. MIV 361
82. MIV 1334
83. MIV 442
84. MIV 523
85. MIV 662
86. MIV 677
87. MIV 574
88. MIV 622
89. MIV 811
90. MIV 823
91. MIII 3480
92. MIV 772
93. MIV 876
94. MV 236
95. MIV 1123
96. MIV 363
97. MVI 57
98. MIV 1322
99. MIII 3089
100. MIV 1436
101. MIV 1444
102. MIV 1488
103. MIV 1596
104. MIV 1516
105. MIV 1353
106. MIV 1649
107. MIV 1652
108. MIV 1656
109. MIII 4010
110. MI 760
111. MIV 1884
112. MIV 1960
113. MIII 4796
114. MIV 1978

115. MIII 1335
116. MIV 1984
117. MIII 4311
118. MV 2504
119. MIV 2052
120. MIII 3511
121. MIV 2062
122. MIV 2120
123. MIV 2140
124. MV 411
125. MIII 4157
126. MIV 2209
127. MIV 2244
128. MII 1734
129. MIV 2350
130. MI 133
131. MIV 2403
132. MIV 2467
133. MIV 2482
134. MV 568
135. MIV 2681
136. MIV 2744
137. MIV 2747
138. MIV 2763
139. MIV 2884
140. MIV 2903
141. MIV 2912
142. MIII 4055
143. MIV 2921
144. MIV 3010
145. MIV 3025
146. MV 1047
147. MIII 4393
148. MIV 3558
149. MIV 3611
150. MIV 3612
151. MIV 3817
152. MIII 2895

153. MIII 4402
154. MIV 68
155. MIII 126
156. MIII 134
157. MIII 213
158. MIII 3488
159. MIII 255
160. MIII 263
161. MIII 267
162. MIII 322
163. MIII 361
164. MIII 371
165. MIII 488
166. MIII 623
167. MIII 745
168. MIII 992
169. MIII 1131
170. MIII 1138
171. MIII 1139
172. MII 3459
173. MIII 1146
174. MIII 1140
175. MIII 1194
176. MIII 1257
177. MIII 1275
178. MVI 3099
179. MIII 1302
180. MIII 1306
181. MIV 1979
182. MIII 1442
183. MIII 1447
184. MIII 1449
185. MI 140
186. MI 215
187. MIV 1318
188. MIII 1506
189. MIII 1538
190. MIII 2061

191. MIII 2257
192. MII 2842
193. MIII 2452
194. MIII 2593
195. MI 3720
196. MIII 2692
197. MVI 1497
198. MI 393
199. MIII 3212
200. MIII 2925
201. MIII 2938
202. MIII 2935
203. MIII 2986
204. MIII 4603
205. MIII 4612
206. MV 1075
207. MI 275
208. MI 283
209. MI 116
210. MIII 4648
211. MIV 1407
212. MVI 2643
213. MIII 3197
214. MIII 3203
215. MIII 3021
216. MIII 3208
217. MIII 4668
218. MIII 3254
219. MIII 3265
220. MIII 3299
221. MIV 713
222. MIII 3355
223. MIII 3444
224. MIII 3474
225. MIII 3448
226. MIII 219
227. MIII 3497
228. MIV 2058

229. MIII 3513
230. MIII 3548
231. MIII 3555
232. MIII 4723
233. MIII 3587
234. MIII 3626
235. MIII 3633
236. MIII 3670
237. MIII 3807
238. MIII 3811
239. MIII 3838
240. MIII 3847
241. MIII 3848
242. MI 1756
243. MI 25
244. MVI 2598
245. MIII 3920
246. MIII 4017
247. MIII 4053
248. MIV 2914
249. MIII 4768
250. MI 611
251. MIII 4121
252. MI 114
253. MIII 4231
254. MIV 2041
255. MIII 4312
256. MVI 134
257. MVI 1978
258. MIII 4401
259. MIV 1340
260. MIII 4418
261. MIII 4511
262. MIII 4516
263. MIII 4621
264. MIII 4733
265. MIII 4735
266. MIII 4769

267. MIV 1976
268. MV 162
269. MV 183
270. MIV 1078
271. MV 236
272. MV 292
273. MV 409
274. MV 396
275. MIV 2169
276. MV 413
277. MIII 124
278. MIV 76
279. MV 498
280. MV 511
281. MV 515
282. MV 526
283. MV 558
284. MV 565
285. MIV 2484
286. MV 569
287. MI 3658
288. MIV 94
289. MIV 112
290. MV 773
291. MV 825
292. MIII 4391
293. MV 1024
294. MV 1051
295. MV 1073
296. MIII 4620
297. MV 1090
298. MV 830
299. MV 871
300. MV 919
301. MIV 113
302. MV 1095
303. MVI 2324
304. MV 1164

305. MV 1168
306. MV 1170
307. MV 1175
308. MV 1310
309. MV 1401
310. MV 1734
311. MI 377
312. MV 1866
313. MI 133
314. MV 1877
315. MV 1941
316. MV 1961
317. MV 2020
318. MV 2116
319. MV 2149
320. MV 2211
321. MV 2346
322. MV 2387
323. MV 2395
324. MV 2457
325. MIV 2051
326. MV 2635
327. MV 2732
328. MV 2900
329. MV 2904
330. MV 3024
331. MIV 1342
332. MV 3130
333. MV 3230
334. MV 3576
335. MV 3696
336. MIII 4118
337. MI 3092
338. MVI 2590
339. MI 1205
340. MI 1882
341. MV 4065
342. MV 4113

343. MV 4117
344. MV 4237
345. MVI 5
346. MVI 8
347. MVI 220
348. MIV 1336
349. MV 1089
350. MVI 408
351. MVI 410
352. MVI 496
353. MVI 498
354. MVI 512
355. MVI 806
356. MVI 812
357. MVI 1267
358. MVI 1356
359. MVI 1407
360. MVI 1481
361. MIII 4596
362. MVI 1591
363. MVI 1592
364. MVI 1967
365. MVI 2611

About the Author

Maryam Mafi was born and raised in Iran. She went to Tufts University in the U.S. in 1977, where she studied Sociology and Literature. While reading for her Master's Degree in International Communications at American and Georgetown Universities, she began translating Persian literature. She lives in London.